WHAT DO I DO... WHEN MOMMY IS GONE?

By

Tanika J. West-Moore
"The Counseling Chef"

This book was gifted to me by God

and is

gifted to you:

_____

By

_____

who just wants to say:

_____

_____

_____

_____

_____

_____

_____

_____

Dedicated to :

First and foremost the QUEEN!!

Adonia Mayette Smith–West MacGoodwin –Smith –West

(inside joke),

My Mother–In Love

Jean Moore,

My God –Mother

Thelma Battle Buckner,

And to my "sister, from another mister"

Adrianne R. Price.

Then, to all of my friends and family who have lost their mothers,

or mother figures. Be they men , women, boys , or

girls. A mother is a very hard thing to lose,

NO MATTER what, and no matter TO WHAT!!!!

Cherish them while you have them!!!!!

Love Always,

Tanika

What do I do When
Mommy is gone, not gone to the
other room,
or gone to the store,

What do I do when
I can't call her on the
phone
and when she is nowhere
to be found,

What do I do when her "don't do thats, don't go theres, they're not your friends, now don't act like thats, I raised you better than thats, respect your elders", and her "I don't care how old you ares" fall on deaf ears because the voice that said them is mute?

6

when her house is no longer my department store, and I can no longer stop by to "borrow" things that I know she actually bought for me?

What do I do when an event that I can't wait to tell her about happens, and she is not here to tell,

9

or I find one of those "My mother would love this" items in the store, but, there is no need to buy it?

What do I do
when all of the things
she reminded me to remember
multiple times, I have to actually
remember because, I can't find
her to remind me of them just
one more time?

What do
I do when I lose
the sound of her voice
in my head and the feel of
her touch on my skin, or that
sweater of mine that she
wore sadly doesn't smell
like her anymore?

14

What do I do
when her phone
number of 20 years
no longer works, and the
voice on the voicemail is
no longer hers?

15

What do I
do When the special
moments that we
used to share, now become
a solo affair?

16

What do I do when mommy is gone, and she was never supposed to leave... at least in my mind? What do I do when I remember that she held me and we talked about my future, but the next day, she wasn't there, and now that I've accomplished it, she is not here to enjoy it with me?

What do I do when I consider how one day, she was healthy and vibrant and then slowly withered away ...all the way ...away?
When I think about the tomorrows that she promised me, but when tomorrow came it was only me?
What do I do???

As I sit alone now looking at my own mortality, and how there may be many more years behind me than in front of me. I remember that we were young together, then we got older, then all of a sudden, you started getting old alone, and now, in this moment, I can see my future through your present.

When mommy is gone... I think...

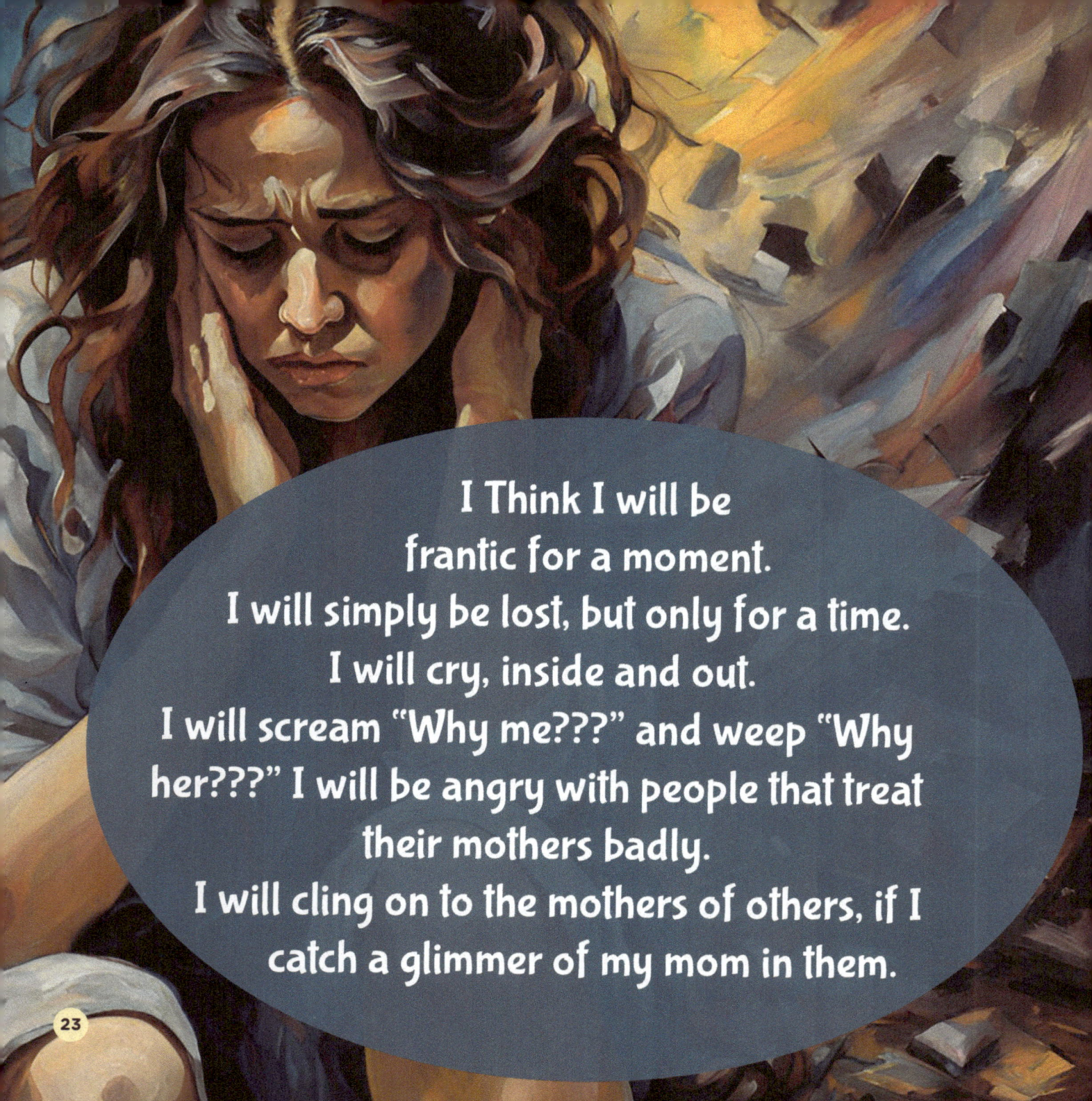

I Think I will be
frantic for a moment.
I will simply be lost, but only for a time.
I will cry, inside and out.
I will scream "Why me???" and weep "Why her???" I will be angry with people that treat their mothers badly.
I will cling on to the mothers of others, if I catch a glimmer of my mom in them.

23

Or maybe, just maybe, I'll be fine...
At least eventually.....

Whatever I am when mommy is gone, is for me to
decide, and no one else to dictate.

I won't feel guilty for how long I cry, or how long I keep her last voicemail, or how tight I hold on to the things that others wanted from her.

26

I won't let time dictate the level or depths of my grief. I will take "me" time in the place of "us" time. I will love myself. I will be kind and forgiving to me.

27

I will overcome the
possibility that, maybe this
feeling lasts forever.
Maybe this is my life for the rest of
my life...
funeral lilies, and sympathetic
looks at Mother's Day Teas.

28

in the
bleach in
my dish water,
or "Lemon Fresh"
mopped floors.
I will find her in the
sounds of old music on
Saturday morning, and
the feeling of the beat in
my heart. I will find her
in the laughter of old
game shows, and
the drama of old
soap operas.

I will hold on to her in the sway of choir rehearsals on Thursday nights, and in concerts and conventions.

I will hear her when I am doing something she told me not to do, in a place she told me not to be, with those she told me meant me no good, and I will leave... Okay, maybe I'll stay but...

I'll definitely hear her words and feel her pushing me to leave and praying for my safe return, and everything about my life.

I will feel her when
I am angry, or sad, happy,
or confused.
I will see her
when I am lost.
I will follow her guidance when
I am lonely and don't know
what to do.

I will forgive
her, represent her,
embrace her, in choices
she made right, and
decisions that she made
wrong. Knowing that both
types of decisions helped
make ME who I am.

34

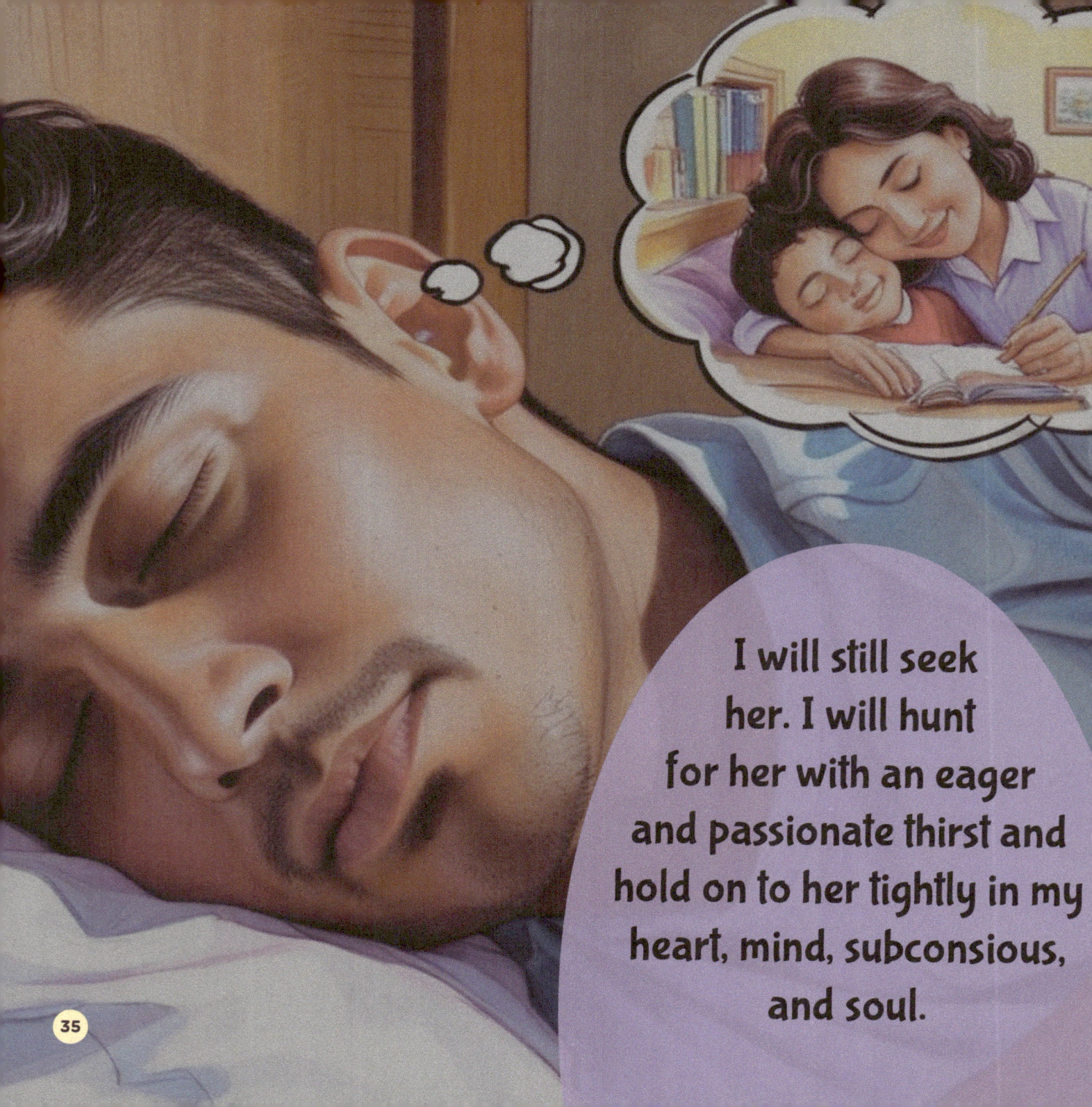

35

I will touch her in the faces of my children or the hands of my friends, knowing that it doesnt get any easier, but it becomes more bareable.

37

And...
I will smile again,
I will dance again, I
will be happy again. And
even though I thought
I could never be me
without her, I will be
a new me!

When Mommy's Gone...

Stages of Grief

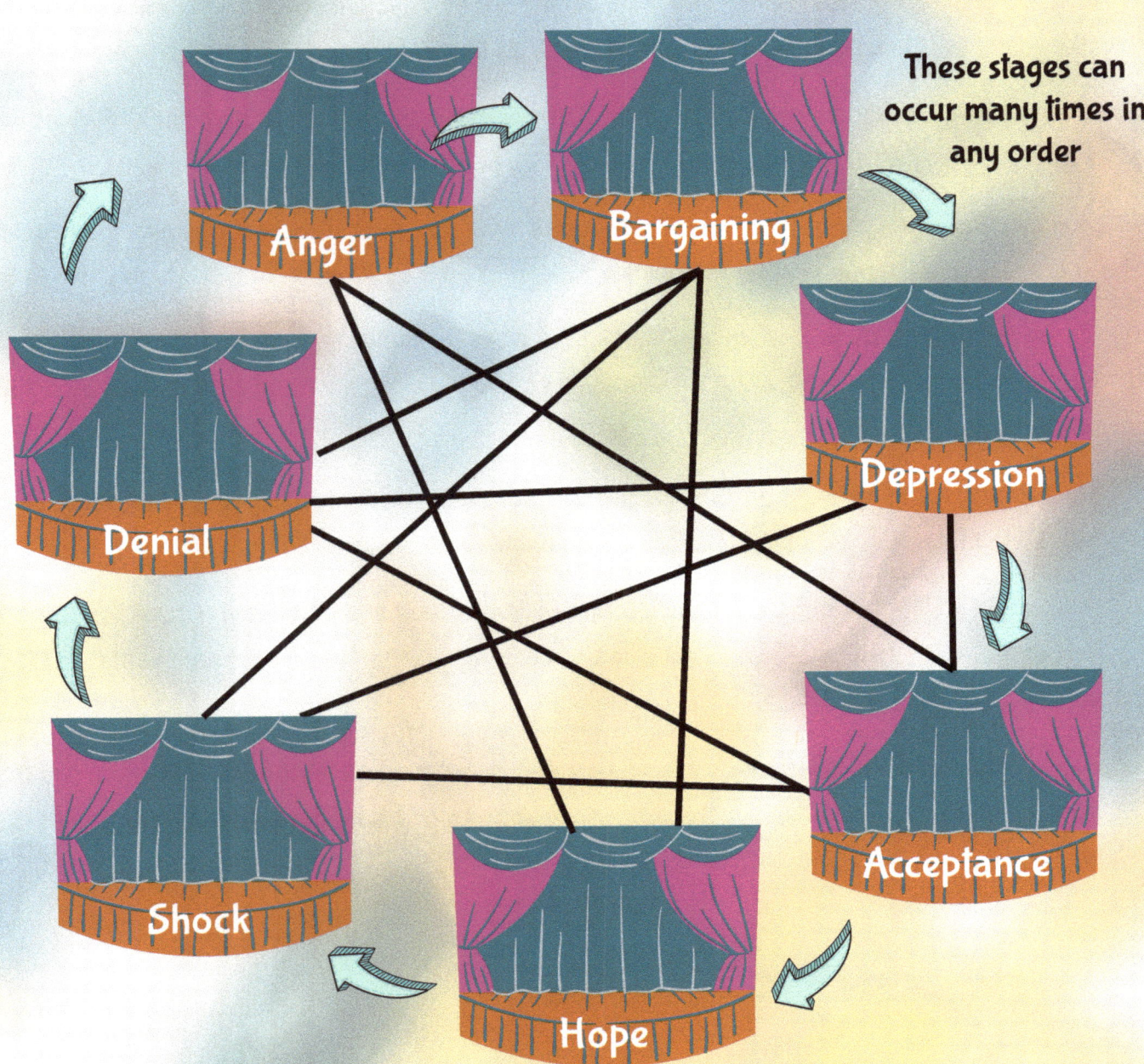

These stages can occur many times in any order

Anger

Bargaining

Depression

Denial

Acceptance

Shock

Hope

40

Shock/Disbelief: This is when you first hear the sad news, and it doesn't feel real. You might feel like you're in a daze, saying, "This can't be true!" It's like waking up from a bad dream.

Denial: After the shock, you might try to act like nothing happened. You might think, "It'll get better soon," or "This isn't really happening," because you're not ready to face the sadness yet.

Anger: Once you start to realize that the loss is real, you might feel really angry. You could be angry at yourself, other people, or even the situation. You may think, "Why is this happening to me?"

Bargaining: This stage is when you think about ways to change the outcome. You might say, "If I had done things differently, maybe it wouldn't have happened." or "Maybe if I make a deal, things will get better."

Depression: This is when you feel really sad or empty. You might cry a lot, feel tired, or lose interest in things you usually enjoy. Everything might seem heavy or overwhelming.

Acceptance: This is when you come to terms with what happened. You understand that the loss is part of life, and even though you're still sad sometimes, you start to feel at peace with it and find a way to move forward.

Hope: After all the sadness and struggle, you start to believe that things can get better. You begin to feel hopeful again and believe that, with time, you can find happiness and strength even though life has changed.

10 Things to remember in grief

1 **You are the only one that can govern how long you grieve.**

Grieving is a personalized experience. You will often find that others may not understand your way of grieving or feel as if you "should" be over it. Realize that relationships between you and your lost loved ones are different than the relationships between others and their lost loved ones. You have personal individual experiences with your love ones that will play integral parts in the grief process. Your experiences with the lost entity, along with your emotional willingness and awareness is what guides your grief.

2 **Be kind to yourself.**

Its hard enough just living life, with no afflictions, or setbacks, but when you add grief on to it, everyday tasks can get hard and you can feel like you are drowning. Sometimes you feel even worse because you feel that you "should" be over it, or "should" be handling it better. During this time be kind to yourself. If you need a minute, take a minute. If you need a day, take a day. Make sure you pour into yourself, make sure you take care of yourself, and make sure you love yourself.

3 **Give yourself grace**

This place called grief may in fact, be a place you have visited before, but you have never been the person you are today, in the climate you are in today, without the person you lost today, and the other out lying factors you have today. This place you are in today is a new place, so give yourself time and grace to navigate through the new.

10 Things to remember in grief

4   Be gentle with those around you.

The people around you may not know what to say or do to console you during this time. They may say things that help, and in turn, they may say things that ABSOLUTELY do not. The truth is that they too are grieving. They are grieving the you of before your loss. All they want is to help you return to that person. Many don't understand that you will never be that person again but you are working through your feelings to get as close as you possibly can. So during your interactions with others show them some understanding as they work hard at attempting to help you stay together.

5   Grief emotions are like change.

Be prepared to experience them anywhere, at anytime, doing anything. At any given time, anything can trigger a feeling or memory that brings your grief emotions to the surface. Grief can sneak up on you and take your breath away. So be kind to yourself during those times, and take the amount of time you need to care for yourself.

6   You have to grieve your losses in a way that is effective for you.

Whether it is a funeral, writing, singing, crying or any other plethora of ideas, your grief is yours. Even if it is nothing, while everyone else is loosing it. It is your choice. There are a few guidelines to this however. As long as you are not harming yourself or anyone else in any way, your grief is a story that you get to write, maybe not from the beginning but you definitely get to determine the end.

10 Things to remember in grief

7 **Grief and loss often do not get better, but they always get different.**

I always cringe when I hear someone say "It will get better", because the truth is we do not know that... at all. What I, and many others can attest to, is that it will get DIFFERENT. Things will hurt less and you will go from missing, hearing the persons voice with agony, to remembering their words when they are needed, with admiration. You will go from possibly crying all the time , to crying only when you are reminded of their importance in your life. But, unfortunately it may never get "better" because this loss will never again not be a loss. I can promise you this, and that is that it will get different. You will cherish the memories, instead of being angry you can't make anymore. You will adapt to your new life, changing into something that can hold the weight of your loss with grace... but you will never be the person you were before.

8 **Forgive yourself and forgive your loved one.**

Sometimes when we don't get to close a relationship with someone before it is not possible to do so, we start exploring regrets and live in a life of "should have's" and "why didn't I's". Or when they leave us without us being prepared, we feel like there are things that are unfinished, and we look for people to blame. Most frequently, it is our selves or our loved one who has passed. Remember, that except for cases of murder, death is no ones fault. The reality is, everything that lives, is going to die. No one can control that.

10 Things to remember in grief

9 **Remember that you are still in control over yourself and your life, you don't need proof.**

Sometimes when we lose someone, to death or otherwise we feel so out of control, and powerless. We search for something that can show us or give us the safety of being in charge of our lives, and our destinies. When we find it, we run into it full steam ahead. It is important that when we are actively grieving we do not make big decisions without the assistance of someone that is levelheaded, clear minded, and that can present to you the pros and cons of the decision. Which brings us to #10

10 **TALK TO SOMEONE.**

Under normal circumstances you may be okay to battle things all alone, but you may in fact need someone else to either guide you or watch over you as you grieve. Be open and honest with the provider share your feelings and your fears. Remember that this is a impartial, honest, open minded, non—biased, and aware person that can help you through this. This person has no expectations but one and that is that you do the work of grief. You can ask your primary care provider, seek a support group, or search for a mental health provider online.

10 Things to do to help with your grief

1. Write a letter to the loved one.

2. Make a play list that reminds you of the good times.

3. Make a donation in the loved one's name to something that you think would be important to them.

4. Use some of your loved one's keepsakes to make an ancestorial alter.

5. Develop a tradition or ritual for holidays, birthdays or anniversaries in the loved one's honor.

6. Learn to cook one of the loved one's favorite dishes or a dish that they cooked well.

7. Plan a trip or to do something that the loved one wanted to do or that you all wanted to do together.

8. Plant a memorial herb garden.

9. Compile a cookbook to distribute to family, that has the loved one's favorite dishes in it.

10. Have a family Roast, where everyone gets together to share funny antidotes about the loved one.

Please consider purchasing the

"What do I do When Mommy Is Gone?" Journal.

The journal was created to accompany this book.